This book is dedicated to Lila Cox, mother and spiritual mentor, who impressed on my young spirit the importance of a close walk with God through hiding His Word in my heart. To my daughter, Kimberly, who edited this work and coached my writing. To my daughter, Kaitlyn, now using her nursing skills at the same place in Thailand where most of these stories took place. And to John, my husband and personal physician these past 45 years.

You are my hiding place; You shall preserve me from trouble; You shall surround me with

Songs of Deliverance.

God promises, "I will instruct you and teach you in the way you should go; I will guide you with My eye."

To request permissions, contact the publisher at admin@TellTheKids.com

Paperback ISBN: 978-1-953935-20-5
Hardback ISBN: 978-1-953935-19-9

Edited by Kimberly Gibson Tran
Cover and Interior Design by Alissa Costello

Scripture quotations marked (ESV) are from The ESV® Bible (The Holy Bible, English Standard Version®), copyright © 2001 by Crossway, a publishing ministry of Good News Publishers. Used by permission. All rights reserved.

Scripture marked NKJV are taken from the New King James Version®. Copyright © 1982 by Thomas Nelson. Used by permission. All rights reserved.

Scriptures marked NIV are taken from the NEW INTERNATIONAL VERSION (NIV): Scripture taken from THE HOLY BIBLE, NEW INTERNATIONAL VERSION ® Copyright© 1973, 1978, 1984, 2011 by Biblica, Inc.™ Used by permission of Zondervan

Published by
Tell The KIDS® LLC
7700 Skylake Drive
Fort Worth TX 76179

TellTheKids.com

Songs of Deliverance

FAITH JOURNEY OF AN AMERICAN NURSE TO THAILAND

LINDA GIBSON

Contents

Humble Beginnings

"In my distress, I cried to the Lord, and He heard me!"

Psalm 120:1 (NKJV)

Allow me to introduce myself: Linda Diane Cox, born exactly on my due date, October 8, 1956, in Corpus Christi, Texas, USA. Many years later in Latin class I realized that, literally, I was born in "The Body of Christ." What an excellent start in life! Since then until present day, I cannot remember a time in my life when I did not love Jesus.

The earliest event I recall from childhood was that, as a toddler in Texas, I wandered from our backyard play area, through a construction zone and past a lake. Mom frantically informed Dad that I had gone missing. Dad's office employees and Mom's friends joined the search. They were calling in the police to drag a net in that lake when Dad found me curled up asleep beside a stack of roofing tiles. I exclaimed to him: "'I cried and I cried 'Help! Help!'" As a small girl I knew the Lord Jesus heard me when no one else could.

That sequence has repeated itself on numerous adventures since then and in that order:

I gave up trying in my own strength.

I cried out to my Father for help.

The LORD heard me and answered!

Shortly after that traumatic event, our family moved to Indianapolis, Indiana, where Dad's chosen profession in manufactured housing and recreational vehicles was booming business. I completed primary and secondary education, graduating in June 1974 in Indianapolis.

My next faith-building experience happened in that city when I was just seven years old.

LESSON

Stop trying in your own strength and call out to Father for help.

Linda's Very Personal Very Scary Halloween Story

*"You are my hiding place; You will protect me from trouble
and surround me with songs of deliverance. I will instruct you
and teach you in the way you should go; I will counsel you
with my loving eye on you."*

Psalm 32:7-8 (NIV)

In 1963 I turned seven years old and started first grade
that October at Chapel Hill Elementary School in Indianapolis, Indiana. Our family of four attended Lynhurst Baptist
Church where Dad served as a deacon. My parents did not
consider Halloween anything other than begging candy from
neighbors while dressed in disguises. So, for October 31st
Dad had purchased tickets to the Holiday on Ice Show at
Indiana State Fairgrounds Coliseum. Several other
families we knew from church were also going to see the

show. It sounded really boring to a seven-year-old and her nine-year-old sister seated in the back of our family's Dodge. So, when we stopped to get gas at the "sign of the flying red horse" (Mobil Oil Station), my older sister Sue and I whispered, "Let's tell them we're sick!" We lied to our parents, said we had tummy-aches and were about to throw up.

Somehow they believed us and abruptly turned aside into the small shopping plaza across the street where we walked a bit, ate a light dinner at a cafeteria, and drove home. We did not get to go trick or treating at neighbors' homes with friends, but were sent straight to bed. I don't even recall any discussion or irritation associated with the decision to skip the Holiday on Ice Show that my mother had wanted to see for a long time.

At 4:00 a.m. my dad received an urgent phone call informing him that several of our church members had been in an explosion at the Indiana Coliseum and four from our church were confirmed dead!

In all, 81 people were killed and 400 injured when several huge propane gas tanks at the concession stand below the seats exploded, throwing people onto the ice. In that same instant, huge blocks of ice and concrete that had buckled came raining down on top of them. We had been spared the horror! To this day, that 1963 explosion is recorded as the worst disaster in Indiana state history.

As I considered the news, it occurred to my child's mind for the first time that:

God knows where I am.

He knows my future.

I can trust Him.

These facts have remained with me my entire life and

have guided many decisions made as an adult. I know that God has a purpose that He intends to fulfill through my life. I will die when He decides and not by chance, nor dictated by karma.

LESSON

I can trust God with life and death matters.

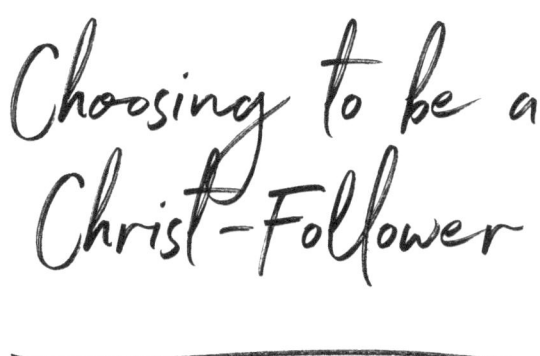

Choosing to be a Christ-Follower

"We were buried therefore with Jesus by baptism into death, in order that, just as Christ was raised from the dead by the glory of His Father, we also might walk in newness of Life.

Romans 6:4 (NKJV)

"If you confess with your mouth the Lord Jesus and believe in your heart that God has raised Him from the dead you will be saved."

Romans 10:9 (NKJV)

As I pondered how God had kept me from that deadly explosion at the Indianapolis coliseum, over the next two years of my childhood, I memorized and recited to my Sunday school teacher the fascinating story of Joseph in the Book of Genesis about how God rescued and spared Joseph for a future, higher purpose. My parents and pastor explained eternal salvation through faith in Jesus Christ, and at a June revival meeting at Lynhurst Baptist Church in Indianapolis, at age nine, I stood up and walked to the front of the packed church to tell the pastor that I wanted to commit my life to being a disciple of Jesus Christ. Weeks later I received baptism at Lynhurst.

Another pivotal point in my ninth year was my first experience with surgery. Drainage tubes had to be placed in my eardrums. After this first experience under anesthesia, I realized a person could fall asleep and have no memory of painful surgery.

My third-grade essay showed my intention to share my faith through medical ministry to the underserved overseas. Anesthesia became my career choice to pursue, and thereafter, God opened every necessary door for me to pursue that vision!

I began to sense that God had also bestowed on me the spiritual gift of mercy. He opened my eyes to find the source of others' pain. The sight of wounds did not upset me. Even as a child, I treated hurting people with tenderness and genuine compassion. Thus began my journey to search out how God had purposed me to relieve some of the suffering in this world.

Looking back, God has used my anesthesia skills to save lives and diminish pain in emergency rooms, intensive care units, and operating rooms in India, Cambodia, Haiti, Thailand, and of course, in the USA.

LESSON

I am saved only by Grace, through Faith in Jesus Christ.

Growing Up on the Indiana Farm

"But when the goodness and loving kindness of Jesus our Savior appeared, He saved us. Not because of works of righteousness that we have done, but according to His own mercy, by the washing of regeneration and renewal of the Holy Spirit.

Titus 3:4-5 (ESV)

Through the late 1960s and early 70s, America integrated races in public schools. This was not a problem in our family because we had not grown up prejudiced against kids of darker skin tones than ours. Since our rural home was the final stop on the way to school, my sister and I got to know African-American kids on the long bus rides, and friendships developed. At church, testimonies by missionaries from Africa and Asia intrigued me! So when my seventh grade Latin teacher asked each student why they chose to study Latin, without hesitation I disclosed to the class that I aspired to a career in anesthesia in order to serve peoples of the world who had limited access to medical care.

Living those pivotal years on a farm, unable even to see the next house down the road, brought quiet solitude that opened my heart to the spiritual presence of Jesus. Perched on the concrete bridge railing of Bridgeport Road, Jesus and I enjoyed long conversations on every subject.

On that bridge, between the ages of 13-14, my Savior Jesus convicted me of selfishness. One day I came to the end of myself and confessed to Jesus how out of control I had been acting. I repented that day and asked God to take control. I was content with newfound freedom to let Jesus, my closest friend, lead me.

At age 16, I broke in my chestnut Arabian filly, Duchess Bonniebee, and biked and camped with my faithful and fearless German shepherd, Harvey at my side. Dad built a two-stall wooden stable at the edge of the woods near the rear of our seven acres of pastureland, as far from the house as possible. "Duchbee," as we fondly called her, shared the stable with my sister's bay Quarter Horse, Bingo.

The pasture gently sloped down to a free-flowing creek that provided drink all year for our pets. The creek and woods allowed unlimited exploration. My high school buddy and I dug a firepit, covered it with a grate, and frequently cooked and camped within the woods' quiet denseness of birch, oak, and maple.

During my freshman year at The Master's College in Los Angeles, CA, I missed the woods and horses sorely. I realize now, far beyond the scope of learning opportunities in college, the spiritual yielding and contentment I found on Bridgeport Road readied me for a lifelong commitment to international missions service.

LESSON

Yield and be content.

15

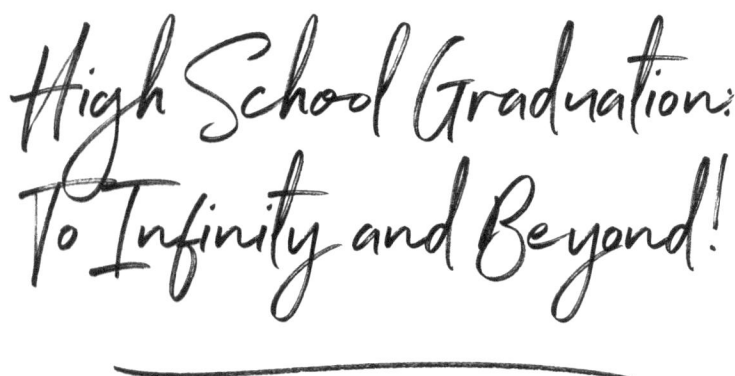

High School Graduation: To Infinity and Beyond!

"In Jesus, you also, when you heard the Word of Truth, the gospel of your salvation, and believed in Jesus, were sealed with the promised Holy Spirit, Who is the guarantee of our inheritance until we acquire possession of it, to the praise of His glory."

Ephesians 1:13-14 (ESV)

Ben Davis High School marching band received the honor of leading the annual Parade of Flowers in that beautiful coastal city of Nice, France. What a grand reception we received! I played the baritone horn not only because of its deep mellow sound, but also because it had a mouthpiece large enough to accommodate those braces around my teeth during 7th and 8th grades.

With its huge bell, my baritone horn took in armfuls of roses and confetti thrown over band members as we marched the parade route that evening. Periodically, we had to turn our instruments upside down to empty them. A reception at the Governor's mansion followed.

The next day found most of us goofing around and cooling off in the aqua waters of the Mediterranean. A day of rest at last! We were fore warned about the high waves of the rocky coastline that day, but our adventurousness took us farther out than we intended.

As I swung around to start back toward the beach, a giant wave engulfed me. Roaring, the waves rolled me until I had no clue which way was up or down. I was heading away from shore in a riptide! Pebbles filled my ears and nose, and my lungs began to burn with the need for air.

In that instant I realized death was close. My detached thoughts said, "I guess this is how it ends for me." I ceased struggling and welcomed God's peaceful presence of comfort around me. I felt surrounded by tranquility.

With the next giant surge a wave spilled me out, right onto the beach! I laid there stunned! Warmed by the sun, I was thankful to live another day at age 17, ears, nose and hair full of pebbles.

This was the first time death's door opened wide to receive me in my younger years.

LESSON

I don't need to fear death because I am sealed by the Holy Spirit.

College Days

And your ears shall hear a word behind you, saying, "This is the way, walk in it," when you turn to the right or when you turn to the left.

Isaiah 30:21 (ESV)

Ben Davis High School was overcrowded, so without hesitation I grabbed the opportunity to graduate a year early and left everything familiar to study at a Christian college in Los Angeles, CA, several states South and West from my Indiana farmhouse. Since I knew no one who attended The Masters College, I felt the freedom to be and become the person God was directing me to be, leaving behind my shy teenage persona.

My sister Sue joined me at The Masters College, but she had not paid for her matriculation fee of $25. Because our parents had little income, as my dad had lost his job, we did not feel that we could ask them for more, so we asked our Heavenly Father.

Just as we sat together in the dormitory lounge, wondering how to pay the college fee, a check arrived that very week! It came from a neighboring farm where Sue had been hired to tend horses and one horse had kicked her thigh. She had not required major medical intervention, so she had not asked the horse owner for remuneration. A lawyer representing the horse farm found us there in California and presented her a check for $250! God sent it just in time!

The final month of that freshman year, The Masters College offered me a scholarship to continue my studies there in the fall, but I had applied two months before to transfer to Baylor University in Waco, Texas, which boasted an outstanding accredited nursing program. The chemistry professor needed an answer before the end of that week so he could request my scholarship.

Immediately, I approached my Lord in prayer, seeking His direction on which path I should choose because only He knew my future. That very week, I received my acceptance letter to study pre-nursing at Baylor University and knew that was where I should go! I transferred to Baylor to begin my sophomore year of college.

Increased tuition necessitated a job, so I took the anatomy lab assistant position and worked for several hours per week, which boosted my knowledge base and served me well later in my nursing and anesthesia studies. Neither of my parents had graduated from college, so the Lord was my guide through all these decisions at age 18.

My existence having begun in Corpus Christi, Texas, it felt as if I were at home among cowboys, kicker dancing, and horse competitions! Ornate and stately Pat Neff Hall housed the Carillon bell tower within its golden dome. Lit up at night in the center of campus, Christian songs and hymns rang out each evening at 8:00 p.m. into every corner and dorm on campus. The bells soothed my loneliness with warm tones of peace carried on each lingering note.

At the end of my sophomore year, I earned acceptance into the Baylor nursing program and moved up to Dallas to complete my BSN. That summer before classes started, I met with the head of anesthesiology at the Baylor Medical Center in Dallas. I learned from Dr. Simpson that a master's degree in Nurse Anesthesia required half the years of study vs. becoming an M.D. Anesthesiologist. And on top of that, a school of Nurse Anesthesia existed in nearby Fort Worth, Texas, and it was free! No tuition required for the whole two years of study!

The summer before my senior and final year at Baylor School of Nursing, Texas Baptists chose me to join a team of university students traveling to Germany, Austria, and Switzerlan! For three months we held Vacation Bible Schools in Baptist churches of several cities, including two youth camps in the Alps. That memorable summer blessed our American military families in Europe while stoking the embers of overseas missionary service that God had placed in my own heart a decade earlier.

LESSON

Commit and Trust God's Plan.

Courtship and Wedding Bells (1979)

"You will go out in joy and be led forth in peace; the mountains and the hills will burst into song before you, and all the trees of the field will clap their hands!"

Isaiah 55:12 (NIV)

As a new Christ-follower, John knew nothing about medical missions. Already a third-year medical student at UT Southwestern in Dallas, John desired courtship, but I solemnly informed him that we need not go that direction if he was not willing to serve God overseas. I was willing to follow God's call to overseas mission service as a single nurse anesthetist.

After reading a few missionary biographies that I loaned

him and personally meeting physicians currently serving in mission hospitals overseas, John felt a nudge from the Holy Spirit. But it took him another six months to convince me that he felt God was calling him to medical missionary service, too.

After another four months of courtship, during which I observed John growing in his new faith in Jesus and genuinely considering medical missions, God allowed John Owen Gibson to intersect my trajectory. We married in the chapel of Wilshire Baptist Church on March 3rd, 1979, in Dallas, Texas.

After a quick honeymoon in Acapulco, Mexico, we both trudged on with work and education. By March the following year, John had served on a disaster relief team after a hurricane in the Caribbean and later traveled on an evangelism team to South Korea where he gave testimony of his personal call to faith and missions in patient wards at the Bill Wallace Memorial Hospital in Pusan.

Together we celebrated our first anniversary on a 3-month med school rotation at Bangalore Baptist Hospital in India. This was full immersion! I was able to minister alongside him in Korea and India. John would later disclose that his call to missions came in India.

While working at Bangalore Baptist Hospital, we both had excellent opportunities for growth in our medical knowledge and skills in areas of tuberculosis treatment, leprosy treatment, surgery and anesthesia.

I learned endotracheal intubation on John's hip replacement surgical patients. Other milestones in that setting were my acceptance letter to the Nurse Anesthesia program in Fort Worth via Aerogram. Two weeks later John marched into the Family Practice Residency program at JPS Hospital in Ft. Worth. We were on our way! God had shown us, there in India, that we could live and work in a low-resource cross-cultural hospital and thrive!

Returning to Texas after three months in Bangalore, India, we moved to Fort Worth to begin the next phases of our training. I graduated after two years of anesthesia training in the fall of 1982. As the top graduate of my class, the didactic achievement award required an acceptance speech. Trembling, I recited Micah 6:8 as my life's verse, my guiding principle: "God has shown you, O man, what is good. And what does the Lord require of you but to live justly, and to love mercy, and to walk humbly with your God."

The spiritual gift of mercy that God bestowed upon me has borne out in a 40 year career of administering anesthesia. Twenty of those years were without pay in a rural Christian hospital in central Thailand and then along the border of Laos in a full scale clinic that welcomed and treated the tribal peoples of Northern Thailand.

Since opium addiction was endemic in those mountain villages where the poppies grew, our clinic bought property nearby and built, from bricks we made on site, a drug rehab in-patient facility. We nicknamed this facet of our care the LOTS ministry, which stands for the Least Of These. This new nursing challenge became my favorite job.

We watched men and women who had been addicted to opium for 20 or 30 years come clean, gain weight, and learn to praise the God who comforts and heals. I enjoyed massaging our drug addicts' backs and legs with Icy Hot ointments to relieve the inevitable muscle cramping.

We saw the Word of God rejuvenate brains through scripture memory and songs of worship! Many were buried with Christ through baptism and raised to walk in newness of life. Former addicts worked the farm there, learned new skills, and returned to their villages with new vigor and seeds of faith.

LESSON

Thrive outside our comfort zone when and where God leads.

Education Finally Completed! (1982)

"For You are great and do wondrous things; You alone are God. Teach me Your way, O Lord; I will walk in Your Truth, unite my heart to fear Your Name. I will praise you, O Lord my God, with all my heart, and I will glorify Your Name forevermore!"

Psalm 86:10-12 (NKJV)

Southcliff Baptist Church hired an interim pastor for six months named Jack Taylor. His goal for those months included teaching us to give generously and to praise God in every situation, bad or good. During Pastor Taylor's time at Southcliff, John felt he should let go of his prized possession—his 1965 Ford Mustang hatchback!

Our answering machine was filled with offers the first weekend after he advertised it. SOLD! John gave the money to the missions Christmas offering to be used for missionaries' needs overseas.

I knew then that he was serious about missions and was

preparing his heart to go. However, the International Mission Board said we needed seminary classes and a minimum of two years' experience in our respective occupations.

One evening I got an urgent call to Johnson County Memorial Hospital. Their Emergency Room had just received three people hurt in a motor vehicle accident, this time in a pickup truck. I hurried to prepare the anesthesia machine in the operating room for a three-year-old girl whose right hand had open fractures on several fingers.

Working alone as a recent anesthesia graduate, I sent up a prayer asking God to watch over us all and guide us. I administered rapid induction intravenous anesthesia and a muscle relaxant. The little girl coughed, then vomited her dinner into her throat and her pulse rate dropped from 110 to 30 beats per minute. She had aspirated stomach acid and food into her lungs!

The surgeon started chest compressions until I could secure her airway with an endotracheal tube and correct her heart rhythm. As he hurried to stitch up the broken fingers, I suctioned copious brown secretions from her lungs—not a good sign. The surgeon did not want to take the time to set the fractures. He wanted to wait until she stabilized.

We transferred the little girl to ICU with the breathing tube still in place, while still suctioning brown secretions from her lungs. But she wasn't waking up! Every anesthetist dreads this situation.

As I drove home from the hospital, Pastor Jack Taylor's words reverberated in my head: "Give praise to God in every situation because He is in control and He has a plan. Rejoice in the LORD in all things." So I began to sing praise songs to God and commit this little girl into His watchcare and to literally thank Him for this scary situation, asking Him to bring glory to Himself through it all.

The next morning, I dreaded calling the ICU for a report on the 3-year-old. "Doing great!" the nurse exclaimed, "We took out her breathing tube, and she is sitting up in bed playing with her father. No cough. No fever."

Two days later, I asked the orthopedic surgeon Dr. Feanne when he would bring her back to the operating room to fix her broken fingers. He replied, "Won't need to. Yesterday the x-ray showed every bone in perfect alignment." We all cheered because every worker in that OR realized what a miracle had occurred before our very eyes! I drove home with a grateful heart and a deeper understanding of our great God.

Rev. Jack Taylor chronicled his 6 months of sermons at Southcliff Baptist Church into a book titled *The Hallelujah Factor*. I bought it.

LESSON

The Hallelujah Factor: Learn to PRAISE in all situations.

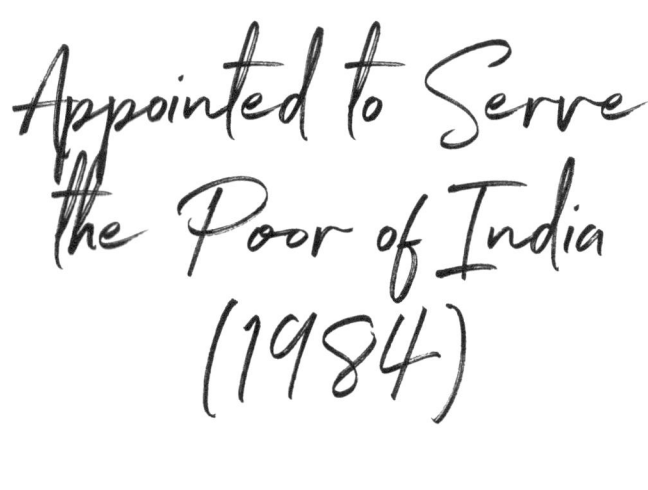

Appointed to Serve the Poor of India (1984)

"For whom He foreknew, He also predestined to be conformed to the image of His Son."

Romans 8:29 (NKJV)

John finished his family practice residency, and we took the next step—we applied to serve under the International Mission Board, with the Southern Baptist Convention, as medical missionaries to India.

We felt God pulling us back to India since our three-month stay in 1980. We had intentionally found Indian friends to help as they stepped into our American culture. We gave them driving lessons, took them bowling, spoke to them about our faith in Jesus, cheered their progress in adapting. And we learned how to cook a few Indian-style foods from these new friends. We felt certain that God was sending us to India.

Planning to be closer to family when we returned from serving overseas, John and I sold our Texas home and moved into a custom-built new house next to my parents' home. Dunnellon, a beautiful, peaceful small town on the crystal-clear Rainbow River in central Florida, became home to us. We completed the required two-month training course for missionary service in Virginia that fall. Near the end of our training there, disturbing news came from India. Prime Minister Indira Gandhi had been assassinated! Riots erupted all over that country—as a result our long-term visas were denied!

We waited in Florida, worked part-time jobs, adrift like our pontoon boat down at the dock. We decided to attend the annual Southern Baptist Convention in San Antonio, Texas, and visit John's mother there while we prayed and waited for our visas to India.

June Gibson, John's widowed mother, never forbid us to go across the world to minister to the poor. However, she had voiced her fear that her only son would be far away taking care of strangers when she needed him most in her elderly years. While living with June that week of the convention, John noticed that his mother was easily short of breath and often complained of back pain. He called her family doctor, whom she had not visited in three years, and made an appointment, quietly telling the nurse on the phone that he suspected lung cancer that was already spreading to her bones. His medical instincts were confirmed the following week by bronchoscopic biopsy and spinal X-rays. John drove straight back to San Antonio and remained at his mother's bedside until she passed into Heaven six weeks later, taking part in her care and helping comfort her.

God gave June Gibson this precious gift of the presence of her doctor son when she most needed him. God's ways are higher than our ways, and His thoughts higher than our comprehension, Isaiah chapter 55 states.

Two weeks after we buried John's mother, a request came from Thailand for a doctor and an anesthetist to join the medical staff serving at Bangkla Baptist Hospital. Without hesistation, not even knowing where Thailand was on the globe, except that it was in Southeast Asia, we accepted that this was where God wanted us to serve Him.

While we waited for the visas to India, which were denied even after a lawyer was sent by the Bangalore Baptist Hospital to request a review in Delhi, I heard a sermon one Sunday night on "the will of God." This message made more sense to me than any previous explanation: "God's will is not a location or a vocation, but that in life's circumstances we might be conformed to the image of His Son Jesus." We stepped out in faith, trusting our Heavenly Father to prepare our way.

The lesson I learned as a seven-year-old child reverberated in my spirit: God knows where I am, He knows my future, and I can trust Him.

LESSON

Learn how to know God's Will.

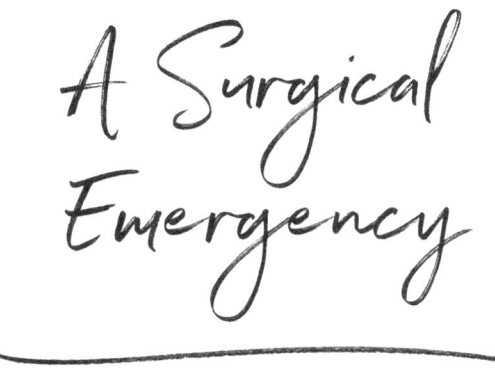

A Surgical Emergency

"For they shall be the descendants of the blessed of the LORD, and their offspring with them. It shall come to pass that before they call, I will answer; And while they are still speaking, I will hear."

Isaiah 65:23-24 (NKJV)

"God is our refuge and strength, a very present help in trouble."

Psalm 46:1 (NKJV)

While waiting for our Thailand visas and airline tickets to join the team at Bangkla Baptist Hospital, I worked at a hospital in Inverness, Florida, not far from our home on the Rainbow River.

My schedule that day in their operating room included a case of total hip revision. That meant taking out the metal hip joint that had previously been inserted and re-doing the whole procedure. All anesthetists know that these cases have heavy blood loss.

The woman was only 40 years of age but had poor health and brittle bones from a long history of alcoholism. She had heart disease and was on two medications that do not allow the heart to speed up even when more blood circulation is required.

During the hip revision, the woman's blood pressure continued dropping despite blood transfusion and intravenous (IV) fluids. Her pulse remained slow and unable to compensate for this rapid blood loss. When the surgeon finished the hip revision, we transported her to the recovery room on an Epinephrine IV drip, a drug which works in two pathways to increase heart rate. But still the blood pressure dropped. Disparaging vital signs led us to start a Levophed IV drip to directly increase her blood pressure while in the recovery period.

Then the anesthesiologist and I walked directly across the street to attend a scheduled meeting at the anesthesia office. Within a few minutes we were summoned back to the post anesthesia care unit with an anxious report from the nurse that they were starting CPR (cardio-pulmonary resuscitation) on the hip revision patient!

Racing back across the street to the hospital, I sent up a prayer for God to direct me in what I should do next. A distinct authoritative order came into my brain, "Give her a gram of calcium!" I repeated that order to the PACU nurse as soon as we entered the room, the anesthesiologist agreeing with my order.

As a gram of calcium was administered IV, I held the woman's head between my palms and prayed for her to live. I promised God that if He would give her life back, I would visit her later and explain His salvation of her soul using the Bible. Immediately, her blood pressure stabilized and that potent IV Levophed drip was discontinued.

Two days later in her hospital room, she and I discussed all these happenings during and after her surgery. Of course, she had been under sedation and did not recall any of those events. She did not comprehend the miraculous turn of events that gave her back her life that day in the post anesthesia care unit, nor did she turn her heart and soul over to God's amazing grace and salvation.

But I knew Who guided me that day to give her exactly what would help her heart to beat again! The Psalmist called it "a very present help in time of trouble." I would sense God's presence guiding me through many tense situations in another operating room on the opposite side of the world very soon. He was teaching me to listen.

LESSON

God is a present help in time of trouble!

New Language, New Culture (1985)

"For if you possess these qualities in increasing measure,
they will keep you from being ineffective and unproductive
in your knowledge of Jesus Christ."

II Peter 1:8 (NIV)

We flew into Bangkok, Thailand, on September 10, 1985, in the midst of a coup d'état military advance taking place just a few blocks from the Don Muang Airport!

Back home in Florida, our parents watched events on television. As they watched, an American reporter-cameraman was shot, and when he fell over, his camera continued to film the military advancing in on the government district offices near Democracy Monument. My parents saw the picture on their screen go sideways and filming continued as the reporter succumbed to his injuries.

In 1985, phone service was sketchy, mostly static. Sending a telegram was the fastest communication across the ocean that divided us, but we did not know how or where to find a telegraph office and no one we encountered spoke English. My parents did not hear from us for 3 weeks, the time it took an aerogram to get to the US.

There were three coup d'etat during our next 20 years in Thailand, and we came to know the song that goes throughout the country by radio when such occurs, informing the entire populace at once, since few had access to television. Local morning news came over a loudspeaker on every town street corner as well.

Our language adventure began for this farm girl newly arrived in Bangkok, population 8 million, a couple of weeks after the coup failed. Owning no vehicle, we were obliged to ride crowded city buses to and from our language school in Bangkok's business district, far from our small, one-bedroom apartment. John, at 6'1", could not even stand up straight in the bus. We quickly learned that the blue buses had A/C and were a bit expensive for locals at 25 cents and therefore less crowded, so we found seats on most commutes. This adventure lasted one year. Fortunately, monsoon rains ended in October, so street flooding receded by November.

Four straight hours per day of Thai language produced major headaches. We got back to our apartment by 12:30pm and went straight to bed. Every. Day. Good thing we didn't have children yet.

Since we only knew a few coherent phrases by November, the mature missionaries assigned to help us navigate life in Bangkok (a pediatrician and a hospital administrator, the Goatchers) insisted that we hire Wasana to cook and clean for us. She needed the job, they explained.

Wasana, a new Christian, was 19. I was 29. Our mentors, along with Wasana's pastor, decided when she would work and how much I would pay her. Wasana and I stood silently staring at each other as this contract concluded since she knew no English and I barely spoke Thai. By her first day in our apartment, I had learned two phrases in Thai language: "Wash your hands first" and "If you are finished, you may go home." Wasana's eyes lit up at that, and she headed for the door!

By the end of our first year, John and I realized that we had learned more Thai language and "street smarts" from Wasana than from our fancy school that only wanted us to speak proper Thai. Wasana moved with us to Bangkla and stayed close until we returned to the States 20 years later. She taught my children their first Thai words, watched over them, and fed us well. For our part, we increased her salary, taught her English, keyboard, computer skills, and baking. At the hospital, she learned nursing aide and laboratory skills.

In 2021, my youngest daughter, Kaitlyn, DNP (Nurse Practitioner), began serving at the Baptist Clinic in Bangkla, Thailand, and Wasana coached her language adventure.

LESSON

Learn Humility and Perseverance.

My First Anesthesia Case in Thailand (1985)

"Come to me, all you who are weary and burdened, and I will give you rest. For my yoke is easy and my burden light."

Matthew 11:28,30 (NIV)

"Have not I commanded you? Be strong and courageous. Do not be afraid; do not be discouraged, for the Lord your God will be with you wherever you go."

Joshua 1:9 (NIV)

Bangkla Baptist Hospital lost its anesthesia provider of 16 years to kidney cancer before we even completed our year of language study in Bangkok. I began receiving calls from the surgeons asking me to drive three hours on weekends to anesthetize children or other patients who could not be operated on using spinal or ketamine-type anesthesia.

My first case was a five-year-old boy requiring splenectomy due to an enlarged spleen from thalassemia major. An enlarged spleen causing pressure on his lungs, plus severe anemia, deemed this necessary surgery a high anesthesia risk for this small child.

As I inspected the operating room and the only anesthesia machine available in this small 35-bed community hospital, the only pediatric-sized equipment I could find was old and re-used hard red-rubber endotracheal tubes with high-pressure cuffs. The type which had been discontinued in the States for several years.

All anesthesia circuits, blood pressure cuffs, intravenous tubing in the OR fit only adult patients. The ventilator, also for adults, was non-functioning, which necessitated hand ventilating each breath for the duration of the surgery. All blood pressure measurements had to be taken by a finger on the child's pulse using a cuff/bulb device.

No pulse-oximeter and using a 16-year-old anesthesia machine that leaked gases in several places meant that I would be inhaling some anesthesia too! "Good thing I brought my weighted chest stethoscope to listen to heart and breath sounds during the case," I said out loud to cheer my growing sense of doom. Totally dependent on my Lord Jesus Christ, I prayed over this pale boy before I even began induction of anesthesia. I asked God to bring this very ill child through this major surgery.

God watched over this little one and answered my specific prayer. The boy came through the procedure and anesthetic just fine.

Beginning with this surgical case and praying over each and every one who required surgery and anesthesia at Bangkla Baptist Hospital, I spent the next three years as the sole anesthesia provider for that entire district which meant being on call 24 hours per day, seven days per week.

LESSON

Depend on God.

Medical Miracles: GOD's Hand at Work!

"Let all who take refuge in You be glad; let them ever sing for joy. Spread Your protection over them, that those who love Your Name may rejoice in You."

Psalm 5:11 (NIV)

"When I am afraid, I put my trust in You."

Psalm 56:3 (NIV)

As the only anesthesia provider in Bangkla and the surrounding district, I was constantly "on call." Runners would be sent out on motorcycles from the hospital to find me in the market, teaching homeschool, even at the beauty salon in the middle of a perm! This was before mobile phones appeared in everyone's hands.

So, no surprise when John and I were called "STAT!" out of Sunday morning worship to Bangkla Baptist Hospital directly across the main street to perform a caesarian section delivery. We found a pregnant woman in full eclampsia, seizing and unconscious. The pick-up truck driver reported that she had been like that the whole six-hour trip from a rural Thai village.

As the nurses pushed her gurney straight back to the operating room, I ran to prepare an induction dose of Sodium Pentathol, a strong intravenous barbiturate (propofol has now taken over as our main anesthetic for induction). I put an oxygen mask over her nose and mouth as I prayed for God to protect mother and baby while I injected this potent IV drug. One dose stopped all seizing, so I injected a muscle relaxant and inserted the endotracheal breathing tube. All of this took less than five minutes as the scrub technician prepared her abdomen for John to immediately deliver her baby via C-section.

As with all C-section deliveries at Bangkla, my other role included resuscitating the baby; suctioning mucous, maintaining the newborn's respiratory status, checking the heart beat, all while keeping the mother asleep and pain-free.

"Lord, did I really sign up for this!?"

But praise be to God, mother and baby recovered well from their ordeal without any permanent detriments. Mother woke up calmly, and no more seizures were noted post-operatively. God is so good, so near and His healing is complete.

During their recuperation at Bangkla, our full-time female Christian counselor visited each patient every day, telling them that missionary doctors and nurses came to Thailand not only to heal, but to explain to Thai people that only Jesus has authority to forgive sins and save a person's soul. Many who experience miraculous outcomes realize that the Christian God is powerful and loves them. Many have trusted Jesus Christ to save them.

Now THAT is what I signed up for!

LESSON

Entrust your trained abilities to God's use.

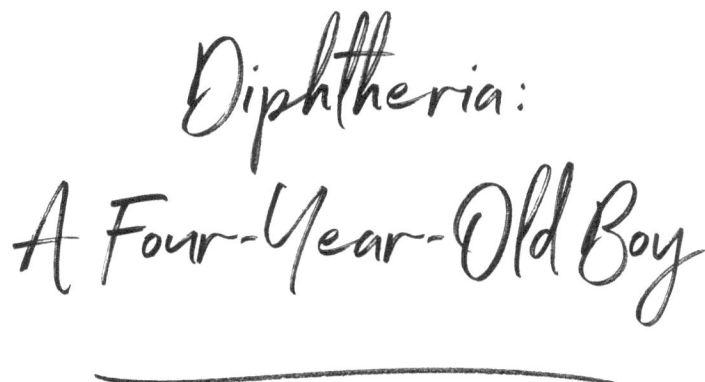

Diphtheria: A Four-Year-Old Boy

"Thus says the Lord Who made the earth, the Lord Who formed it to establish it; Call to Me and I will answer you and will show you great and hidden things that you have not known!"

Jeremiah 33:2-3 (ESV)

A small four-year-old boy sat hunched over in his hospital bed, barely able to suck in each breath. Dr. Butcher already suspected that this young fellow's airway was obstructed by that spreading grey membrane he saw on exam. That is why he had consulted me. In order to save the child's life, Dr. Butcher planned to place a tracheostomy into his throat to bypass the blockage. He asked me to give the little boy general anesthesia to keep him still and without pain during the procedure.

Most of us have been immunized against this dreaded infection since early childhood, so in America, John and I had never seen a case of diphtheria. But Dr. Orby Butcher had helped plant Bangkla Baptist Hospital in 1963, over

20 years before John and I arrived to help him. Diphtheria bacterial infection, not uncommon to diagnose at that time, most likely starts with untreated tonsilitis that spreads into surrounding throat tissues and causes the growth of a tough, thick membrane that walls off the infected area, but it can also close off the entire throat and airway.

This disease presented a major anesthesia challenge-securing an airway that I could not visualize with a laryngo-scope! As I hurried to the operating room, I asked God to guide me and give me wisdom to help save the boy's life.

Since the child could not breathe at all lying flat on the operating table, I held him in a sitting position while I placed an anesthesia mask over his nose and mouth and turned on oxygen and halothane gases.

My goal: to anesthetize the boy deeply enough to get a breathing tube into his trachea while he was still breathing on his own. My physician husband John, who had also never treated a case of diphtheria airway obstruction, asked to look into the throat. John backed away quickly, admitting he could not identify any normal anatomy because of that thick, gray membrane stretching across this little guy's throat.

As always, this case began with prayer for our Lord's guidance. As I placed the scope into the small mouth, God enabled me to see a tiny bubble of air retreat into the membrane. I followed that bubble with an endotracheal breathing tube—and we were in! Giving praise to the Almighty, Who shows us great and hidden things that we didn't know before, Dr. Butcher was able to perform the life-saving tracheostomy. When the operation was completed, the little guy woke up breathing easily.

The tracheal tube remained in place for six weeks until the membrane receded, and the boy's trachea could be properly closed. His parents got to take home a boy they did not think would survive another day. As for me, as soon as the operation was completed, I hurried to the nurses' station and requested a diphtheria booster!

LESSON

Depend on God's Wisdom.

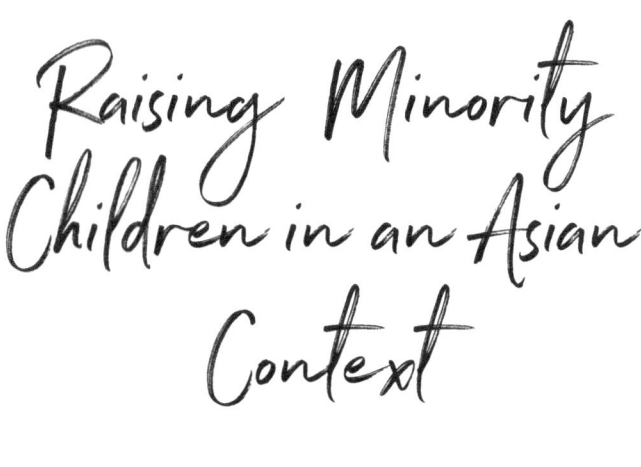

Raising Minority Children in an Asian Context

If you really fulfill the royal law according to the Scripture, "You shall love your neighbor as yourself," you do well; But if you show partiality, you are sinning and are convicted by the law as transgressors.

James 2:8-9 (ESV)

After living and working at Bangkla Baptist Hospital four full years, we were due for a furlough back to the U.S. to visit family and friends. The Bangkla Hospital had sent one of their finest nurses, Chuy, to a nurse anesthesia one-year course of study with application in a large Bangkok hospital. She returned to take my position just four months before we flew to the States.

I had just conceived and could no longer enter an operating room that used nitrous oxide heavily and whose gas scavenging system I had rigged myself. But I was nearby in case Chuy had any questions. Perfect timing, Lord!

Kimberly Dawn was born in Ocala, Florida, during that first furlough. I felt her move for the first time on our long jet ride crossing the Pacific Ocean. Later, Kimberly would describe to me that all she knew of her world was two countries of contradictory cultures, different languages on opposite sides of the Earth. She remembers boarding planes in the dark of early dawn then waking up to totally different surroundings.

Kimberly was 5 months old when we whisked her away from America to the land we had come to love and call "home". She had blond hair and brilliant blue eyes and very white skin. This newcomer caused a stir in town. In the market, a Thai woman waved her hand before Kimberly's strange blue eyes and asked, "Is she blind?" Another woman wanted to know how her hair could turn gray at such a young age!

While we were in the States, Wasana, our beloved cook and housekeeper of four years acquaintance, had taken nurse aide training and would be spending most of each day working on the hospital ward and later in the lab as a technician.

Due to the possibility of a cobra slithering across the back yard and rabid dogs on the loose, we hired a 20-year-old Thai nanny to be an extra set of eyes on our little joy.

Having a child in the home required adjustments to our hospital routine. John and I could no longer be on call the same nights. I adjusted my schedule in the Bangkla Hospital operating room to part time, which translated into two 24-hour shifts per week instead of seven.

A second blond named Kaitlyn Diane returned with our

family after our second furlough. I was 36 years old. The girls grew up bi-lingual and, when each turned three years of age, rode behind me on a motorcycle to a local Catholic pre-school to learn the Thai alphabet and how to count and to make Thai friends. In Thailand, motorcycle helmets come in pre-school sizes!

Designated the only "Farangs" (white foreigners) in their respective classes, our daughters were white specks among the sea of black-haired, brown eyed, brown skinned students, all of whom were on the same human level of wanting to be home with their mothers.

A designation for children raised in a foreign land is "Third Culture Kids". These TCKs are highly adaptable to unusual surroundings and quite accepting of people who don't look or speak as they do. Fourteen years after bringing our first-born daughter to Asia, our TCKs entered Texas public high school unaware of the racial politics and bias endemic to the U.S.

Kimberly obtained a master's degree in English and linguistics, having also learned Spanish before high school graduation. She went on to coach many students of first-generation immigrants to excel in writing essays and resumes and in taking college entrance exams. Kaitlyn obtained a doctorate as a nurse practitioner and returned with her husband Caleb to Thailand to work in the Bangkla Baptist Clinic and share the Good News of salvation through trusting in Jesus Christ with patients she treats there.

LESSON

Embrace the commonality of all humanity.

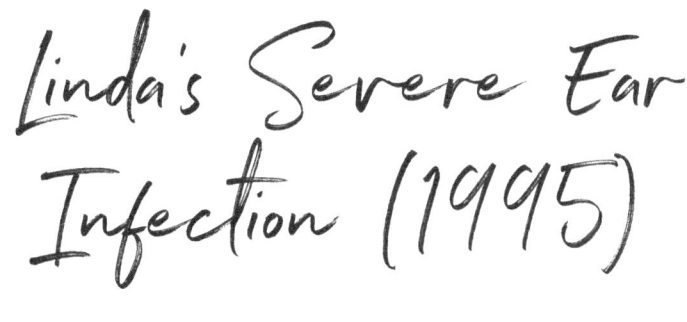

Linda's Severe Ear Infection (1995)

*"And the prayer of faith will save the one who is sick,
and the Lord will raise him up."*

James 5:15 (ESV)

None of us understands why some prayers for healing are answered and why many are not. I found it especially difficult to understand why God chose to heal several Buddhists at our hospital but did not answer some appeals for Christian brothers and sisters. I mentioned earlier the chronic middle ear infections that sent me to surgery twice at age nine and which informed my young mind about the important services that anesthesia providers offer their patients.

During my nursing education, both of my ears plagued me with repeated infections. When I landed my first nursing job and had my own health insurance, I located an ear-nose-throat (ENT) surgeon who repaired both ruptured eardrums with skin from behind each ear. Simple tympanoplasty effectively served my needs for the next 15 years. But serving in a hot, humid climate in Southeast Asia awakened the infection in my left ear. After repeated rounds of antibiotics and trips to a Thai ENT doctor who suctioned out the pus every week, I asked my mission colleagues to pray over me for healing at our annual Thailand Baptist Mission meeting in Pattaya. Nothing happened.

An American ENT surgeon I knew personally and highly respected lived and worked in Singapore at a state-of-the-art facility with a high-powered microscope. He suggested I get a CT scan of the left ear and skull to bring to him in Singapore. Our next scheduled mission meeting would be in Malaysia and afforded me an opportunity to get to Dr. Jim Smith's office in nearby Singapore! Meanwhile, the ear drainage continued.

In anticipation of Dr. Henry Blackaby's teaching visit to Thailand Baptists on "Experiencing GOD", the committee asked me to prepare an interactive prayer guide for our missionaries the months preceding his arrival. Preparing our hearts to hear God's message from this renowned pastor, I fasted one day each week as I wrote up the prayer guide. Because my daughters were toddlers, the only quiet time in my house was between 10p.m. and 6a.m. Even so, the huge fruit bats, for which Bangkla is famous, squawked and flapped their big wings amid the tall trees in our backyard.

Spreading my Bible and commentaries around me at the large dining table, I wrote far into the night for three consecutive nights using the biblical text from Daniel chapters nine and ten. This prayer guide was divided into three, seven-day sections (Prayers of Confession, Praise, Petitions) to comprise 21 days of prayer mirroring Daniel 10:1-13.

During the writing of this prayer guide, my ear dried up for the first time in many months, but I did not realize the significance of a dry ear until Rev. Henry Blackaby stood to speak at our first meeting. His first words at the podium were, "When was the last time you read and meditated on Daniel chapters nine and ten?" Hairs standing up on my arms, eyes brimming with tears, I leaned over to remind John that those were the Bible chapters the Lord had put on my heart months before!

Indeed, Dr. Jim Smith, the ENT surgeon I visited in Singapore confirmed microscopically that not only was my left ear dry, but the huge hole in my eardrum completely healed without any evidence of a year of chronic infection! Praise be to God for this significant healing and for the faith in His power and goodness that welled up inside of me that day.

Twenty-five years later, living back in the United States, my left eardrum ruptured again, this time requiring mastoidectomy, tympanoplasty, and a bone patch to my temporal cranium. I am grateful to have found a Neurotologist in my city of residence (only 200 of those surgeons in the entire U.S.) who put in three hours of tedious and delicate work to repair the damage of yet another full year of purulent left ear infection.

When my options in Thailand were limited, years before these techniques became available to ear surgeons, the Great Physician repaired it overnight and left no scars.

LESSON

Miracles observed through meditation and fasting

Dengue Fever!

"In peace I will lie down and sleep; for You alone, Lord, make me dwell in safety."

Psalm 4:8 (NIV)

Mosquito bites can bring devastating diseases, one of which is common in Thailand's rainy season—dengue hemorrhagic fever. 1994 became a record year for severe cases. Thirty-five patient beds made up our small Bangkla Baptist Hospital, but 55 patients overflowed into the long hallway that summer. Severe reactions to the virus brought hemorrhaging patients from outlying poor provinces to seek our care.

There are four sub-types and most Thai people experience one or several of these while growing up. Wooden houses perch on stilts to prevent flood waters from entering. The houses have wooden shutters but no screens on their windows. Most families share a giant mosquito net to sleep beneath but are otherwise unprotected.

As we sat in Sunday worship at Bangkla Baptist Church, I fidgeted in the pew beside my young family. My heart rate was fast, and I could not sit comfortably. I felt feverish, so

I leaned over and told John. He had two questions for me: 1) Do you have a sore throat? And 2) Do you have a runny nose? My answers to both were "no". He gazed sadly at me and pronounced, "Then you have dengue." Dr. John, as everyone in Bangkla fondly called my husband, had become an expert on tropical diseases in one month! Our ICU had already lost two children to hemorrhage as well as one young lady and one older man, all from dengue fever. And now I was infected!

"Bone break fever" is a common nickname for dengue. We had heard what that felt like from several senior missionaries serving in Laos and Thailand. Some had suffered with joint or bone pain for six months. With no room in our hospital, and my inability to lie comfortably on our waterbed, I took to a firmer twin sized mattress on the floor of our bedroom, and John sent nurses over every four to eight hours to check my vital signs. My legs swelled to twice their normal size and glowed bright red like a second-degree sunburn as my capillaries (smallest blood vessels) leaked into surrounding tissues. Gradually, my blood pressure crept lower. One night several days into this viral disease, I felt my blood draining away. And I felt utter peace. Like Jesus was holding me and I had nothing to fear. I knew I could die but felt no anxiety at all. And no pain. Calmly, I reached up in that dark room and pulled on John's big toe from my low mattress. "Please, can you take my blood pressure?" I could barely croak out the question in my weakened state.

Now it was his turn to panic! Blood pressure reading of 60/0 awakened him to action. As he dressed to drive to our hospital to pick up IV fluid bags and an angiocath to administer those through, I begged him to bring a nurse to start my intravenous catheter. I wasn't sure doctors were very good at that—sticking needles into veins. But he came back alone and did the job quite nicely. I don't even remember the sting. John proceeded to hang IV fluids from the canopy of our bedframe—five liters in all, until he was satisfied that I would live.

Nowadays, 30 years later, I tease him that because he saved my life, he is stuck with me 'til death do us part!

No one warned me that due to lack of peripheral capillary blood flow, I would slough off the skin from soles and palms. The itch aggravated me to the point of taking a hairbrush to scratch off the dead skin. But then new baby-like skin grew back in its place, and that fascinated me to watch.

I will never forget the peace that Jesus brought to my sickbed. No need to fear death, He is always near.

LESSON

There is no fear in death (Jesus brings Peace).

A Boy on a Bike in Bangkla

Many twelve-year-olds learn to drive motorcycles in Thailand, sort of a "coming of age" thing. In 1988, motorcycles comprised the majority of traffic in our town of Bangkla. Accidents happened routinely, almost weekly. Two motorcycles colliding could bring six trauma patients to our ER (emergency room). The greatest number of people I have photographed on one motorcycle is seven: Dad, Mom, and their five children in front of, back of, and standing in between the parents on a standard 120cc Honda. Our own family eventually owned three Hondas, the largest being a 250cc Honda Rebel that John drove to and from work. I taught both of our daughters to drive a motorcycle when they each reached age twelve.

Not surprisingly, I received an urgent phone call one evening from Head Nurse Juri that the hospital ER had triaged a twelve-year-old boy whose "brains are coming out his forehead!" Joyriding on his father's motorcycle, this naughty boy had nearly decapitated himself! We never heard what he ran into on the bike. Quickly arriving at the hospital (less than five minutes' drive from my house), I asked the nurse where the boy had been taken. "He is in X-ray," she replied over her shoulder as she hurried to get blood from the hospital's mini refrigerator.

I found him sitting by himself, legs dangling over the side of the X-ray table, IV in place running at maximum flow, bleeding profusely. He was conscious! He and I spoke briefly about his health history, allergies to medicines, last meal he had eaten--the sort of things that anesthetists are keenly interested in. Then I raced over to the operating room and set up my anesthesia supplies.

Once our small boy was asleep and his airway secured, our Thai surgeon Dr. Jirachat prepped, excised, and debrided the skull and brain as I attempted to get enough blood into this patient. Unfortunately, blood products only came in glass bottles, which cannot be squeezed!! With much difficulty I tried to replenish his blood loss with bottles of donated blood. And I cried out to my Father for help! In our hurry to stop the bleeding, I had no time to meet his parents, nor get an anesthesia permit signed. Somehow rural Thailand did not seem to have a problem with that mode of operation. Just as I had adapted to other cultural norms, I grew accustomed to this M.O.

I teased Dr. Jirachat that since he performed a frontal lobotomy, this little guy would no longer give his parents any trouble. Despite Dr. Ji's protest to the contrary, on follow-up visits to our hospital, this young fellow presented a more subdued demeanor. I'm not sure if he ever rode another motorcycle, but he lived through his ordeal and actually recovered pretty well.

Having no CT scan capabilities in the whole district of Bangkla, we started transporting some of our neuro (head trauma) cases to the next province, which boasted a neurosurgeon on staff. He mailed us a terse reply that he was swamped with cases and implored us to do the best we could with what we had!

LESSON

God is all-sufficient to meet every need.

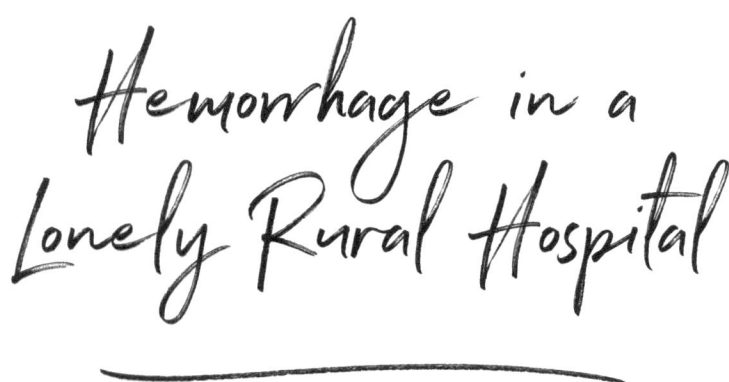

Hemorrhage in a Lonely Rural Hospital

"Nevertheless, I am continually with You; You hold my right hand, You guide me with your counsel, and afterward You will receive me to Glory. Whom have I in heaven but You? And there is nothing on earth that I desire besides You. My flesh and my heart may fail, but God is the strength of my heart and my portion forever."

Psalm 73:23-26 (ESV)

There is no easy access to blood products of any type in Thai rural hospitals, but our lab kept some in a small refrigerator for emergencies. The Red Cross Blood Bank was three hours away in Bangkok.

When a middle-aged woman presented in our Bangkla out-patient department, needing an inflamed and non-functioning kidney removed, I asked our surgeon, Dr. Jirachat, if he thought I should go after more blood. Since he planned to excise the whole kidney all at once, he explained that he did not see the need to track down a blood donor. At that time during our tenure at Bangkla, the hospital maintained a list of townsfolk considered low risk for communicable diseases to be called in to donate blood for emergency use. During the AIDS epidemic in Thailand in the 1980s, this practice was only for extreme emergency situations and soon abandoned as risk increased in our local population. This woman had an uncommon, but not rare, blood type of B+ (B Positive).

That afternoon we rolled the woman back to our operating room and I put her to sleep while Dr. Jirachat scrubbed his hands up to his elbows. Immediately after incision he realized that the non-functioning kidney had festered into surrounding tissues, complicating its extraction. Trying to delicately separate the kidney, blood was lost, accumulating in the suction container on the wall! As the surgeon was having a tough go of it, I calculated her total blood volume based on lean weight and estimated blood lost as a percentage that showed she needed to begin receiving a transfusion. Thankfully, our little fridge in the lab held two units of type B+ packed red blood cells. Over time, she received both units intravenously, but still her blood pressure continued to decline.

When her condition looked precarious, and the wound continued leaking blood into our suction cannister, I gave Dr. Jirachat a stern warning that he needed to slow the blood loss and close her wound as soon as possible. He agreed, but knew that she would not be cured unless he could excise the kidney and the abscess around it. Slowly, I began backing off my anesthesia drugs to maintain her blood pressure. Finally, I informed the surgeon that I would have to completely turn off all anesthesia gases. Even vasopressor meds were not keeping her vital signs in a safe range.

At wit's end, I remembered that if I gave up trying to save this woman in my own knowledge and ability, and cried out to my Father for help, that He would answer! At the very moment I cried out to God for help, my physician husband John poked his head in the door. He noticed how long we had been in the operating room and wondered what kind of predicament we had gotten into. His only words were, "Is there anything I can do to help?"

Immediately, I remembered that John had type B+ blood! I sent him to the lab, and he donated two more units of his own blood, leaving himself a bit dizzy. God had sent me exactly what this woman needed to survive—fresh whole blood, which is full of natural clotting factors and already at body-temperature! She survived and recovered well from her operation.

Our lady evangelist Khun Chavee visited at her bedside daily until she was discharged. She always teasing the Buddhist that half her blood was Christian! She shared that she needed to give her life to Jesus, Who is always ready to save.

LESSON

Cry out to God Who is always listening.

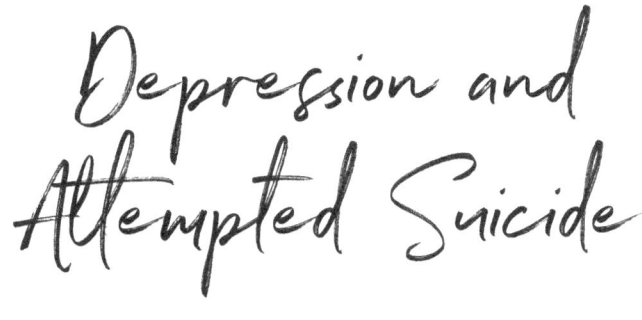

Depression and Attempted Suicide

"For with
God nothing will be impossible."

Luke 1:37 (NKJV)

In many countries, existence is challenging with warring factions, limited resources, lack of education, low wage jobs, human trafficking, and domestic violence. Hopelessness causes people to hurt themselves, and we, as healthcare workers, receive these traumatized people into our hospitals after attempted suicide.

One way many people in Thailand chose to kill themselves was by drinking paraquat (Gramoxone), a defoliant used by farmers on their fields. It literally burns you from the inside out—a painful way to die. Doctors know no way to reverse the effects once it shows up in a urine test. We had yet to see a person attempting suicide in this particular way ever live through it.

When Somchai presented at our hospital emergency room saying he had ingested Gramoxone, Dr. John admitted him to the ICU and tested his urine. Somchai was remorseful that he had swallowed the poison, saying he and his mother had argued about his girlfriend and he wanted to "get back at her." Now he was not feeling well and was hoping we could reverse the effects.

Doctor John sat at Somchai's bedside explaining that once this particular poison was found in urine samples it could not be reversed. But then Dr. John explained the hope that we as Christians have through Christ Jesus our Savior. He told the 19-year-old that through the blood sacrifice of Jesus on a cross, God provided for us to have our sins forgiven allowing eternal admittance into Heaven, where all troubles and tears are wiped away. The teen desired that certainty. John led him in a prayer of repentance and dependence upon Jesus' mercy and grace. Somchai's family lived a long distance away, and John feared that this young man might die alone, so he asked the nurses to call him when the patient's condition deteriorated so that John could come sit with him.

When the nurses had not called Dr. John all night, John awoke with the fear that he had let Somchai down, that he had died alone. He hurried into work and was relieved to see the teen sitting up in bed. The boy was hungry and asked for something to eat. John re-checked his urine, and it was clear! There was no sign of Gramoxone poison in the urine test, and the teen's liver functions had returned to normal as well.

God had saved Somchai's soul and his body. He had been given a second chance at life. This round he was determined to put God before his angry emotions. He returned home changed and truly alive in body and spirit.

LESSON

Nothing is Impossible with God.

Raised from the Dead!

*Jesus cried with a loud voice, "Lazarus, come forth!"
and he who had died came out of the tomb.*

John 11:43 (NKJV)

Sometimes at Bangkla Baptist Hospital, I was asked to translate for visiting volunteer doctors in the outpatient clinic. One of those days, I walked through the empty triage room just as a middle-aged man walked up the wheelchair ramp carrying his dead wife in his arms! No pulse, no respirations! I kicked into anesthetist mode and quickly intubated her trachea with a breathing tube and began to ventilate for this woman. Dr. Sompon walked into the triage room just as all this transpired, and I conscripted her to start chest compressions. We shouted for other doctors behind us in their exam rooms to come out and help us.

The woman's husband watched us work and explained the situation in detail. "My wife was electrocuted by our refrigerator just now! I was upstairs and heard a crashing noise from downstairs. She could not let go of the refrigerator, so it fell on top of her! I pushed the refrigerator off of her and picked her up and put her in my truck and drove here to your hospital!" His words came out in a rush. I assumed he lived in Bangkla and had arrived in just a few minutes after the electric accident, but no one knew how long this woman had been without oxygen or blood flow to her brain. If fewer than five to six minutes had transpired, there would be a chance that she might recover with no brain damage.

As we continued CPR, her EKG showed Ventricular Fibrillation and I called for the hospital's only defibrillator. Then my husband Dr. John rattled us with the astonishing statement that he had used the defibrillator two weeks before in our ICU and that smoke had billowed out of it and the inner parts were "fried."

A visiting pastor, of now-retired missionary doctor Alton Hood, asked where the machine was kept. He said he would begin praying and demanded that someone go get that machine. Dr. John wheeled it in from the nearby administrator's office, where Khun Supachai stored the defibrillator while we waited for "Lottie Moon" offering funds to purchase a replacement.

Pastor kept praying as others joined in pleading with God to show His mercy and strength for this woman and also for the only piece of equipment that would be able to shock her heart back into a normal rhythm!

We hooked her up to the electrodes, the "fried" machine lit up, and we shocked her heart three times. The woman began to breathe on her own and her heart pulsed again! Since she might have brain damage from her ordeal, we put her into our small four-bed intensive care unit with a large window for the nurses' station to keep a close watch on her progress.

The following morning, our patient was awake and knew her surroundings and asked to be discharged to her home since she felt well. She had no neurological damage!! What praise erupted in that ICU among doctors and nurses on their morning rounds!

A week after her discharge, Dr. Sompon and I decided to visit and find out what all she remembered and to pray with her. We found their home on the outskirts of Bangkla, at least eight to ten minutes drive from the hospital! Realizing it must have taken her husband three to five minutes to just carry her to his truck, and the brian is death by six minutes without blood and oxygen, we began to share with her all these events and what a miracle had taken place for her to be alive again!

She had no recall, of course, of anything after being electrocuted until she woke up perfectly normal in our ICU. She had no interest in our Gospel message of hope, either. We left with a deep sadness.

It used to bother me that God had "wasted" raising a Buddhist from the dead—wasted His miracle of healing both on a machine and a fibrillating heart and a hypoxic brain. But I forgot about the second half of this woman's ordeal.

Her husband spoke to everyone he knew of his eye-witness account of events that transpired the day that he found his wife dead under a refrigerator and drove her to the Christian's hospital. Just like we read in the biblical account of Jesus raising Lazarus from death, all who witnessed the event spread the news far and wide. God has His ways of making Himself known to anyone who has ears to hear.

LESSON

Jesus is the Resurrection and the Life.

New Work, New Province, New Skills Required

> "This Book of the Law shall not depart from your mouth, but you shall meditate on it day and night, so that you may be careful to do according to all that is written in it. For then you will make your way prosperous, and then you will have good success."

Joshua 1:8 (ESV)

From 1998 until 2004, our young family ministered among hilltribe villagers in the Thai Province of Nan not far from the Lao border. A full-scale, full-service medical clinic was built by Kasem Naowaophat and his construction team to Dr. John's specifications. We provided a pharmacy, laboratory, X-ray, minor operations, and dental services plus three examination rooms. Kasem's team also built our house and adjacent to us the nurse-aides' dormitory.

Meanwhile, we surveyed Nan, marking Hmong, Mien, and Thai Lue villages on the district map for future mobile clinics to underserved mountaintop peoples who, for the most part, had never heard the name of Jesus. Some villagers had never seen Westerners.

Opium addiction was pervasive and sucked the strength of a high percentage of tribal men and women. The valleys where the majority lived, tended toward amphetamine abuse and alcoholism. Demon priests acted as local healers. Most villagers were in debt to those priests who treating fevers, illness, crop productivity with chants, animal sacrifices and other practices such as beating the fever out of you with sticks. Their centuries-old Chinese remedies afforded nothing for rabies, encephalitis, or seizures.

Again, prayer and fasting became a weekly discipline for me as I led the Mien ministry team. We had 42 villages mapped out to reach with the Gospel of Jesus Christ. We began, with permission from Thai public health officials and individual village headmen, to hold two or three day mobile clinics to assess needs and begin initial treatments for chronic disorders, which were then referred to our central Chiang Klang Christian Clinic for follow-up.

Local needs were assessed and treated, then we scheduled follow up visits to bring additional medications and teach the Word of God more deeply. In nearly every village people responded to the Gospel message that we preached, acted out in skits, and sang about. New Believers usually discarded or even burned all of their demon worship paraphernalia. Many signed on for drug rehabilitation. Most desired baptism and gathered into church groups.

Missionary kids, helped by giving out dental hygiene kits, holding a flashlight for the doctor or dentist, distributing food and candy and making balloon animals for a crying child. They also performed puppetry to Thai songs and acted out skits about Grace vs. Karma! They rarely complained about camping in tents and getting cold bucket showers, they soldiered on with us.

Rainy season made it a bit tricky on the muddy mountain roads even in my 4WD Mitsubishi Strada. One such follow-up village visit ended with a thunderous downpour. My team included three nurse-aides named Boom, Maan, and Sai. We agreed that we should head back down the mountain before mud became too thick to navigate. Wheels coated with red clay, we progressed until we could see the paved road that led home.

As I turned the steering wheel at the last hairpin turn, our truck slid toward the edge of the mountain! No guard rails existed. All three nurse-aides gripped the doorknobs to jump if the truck listed. I attempted the turn again, but the truck slid closer to the cliff edge. Putting the truck in neutral, with my foot firmly on the brake, we began singing praises to our Lord for His watchcare over us. "Jehovah Jireh, my Provider, Your grace is sufficient for me. You shall give your angels charge over me. Jehovah Jireh cares for me!"

After our short praise offering, I put the truck in gear and the tires found a grip. We turned and lumbered up the final ascent onto paved road. Hallelujah! The storm had blown trees over and we had to get out to clear debris so we could pass, but we were all smiles, basking in the loving care and protection of our Savior Jesus Christ.

LESSON

Fear not the perils of this world.

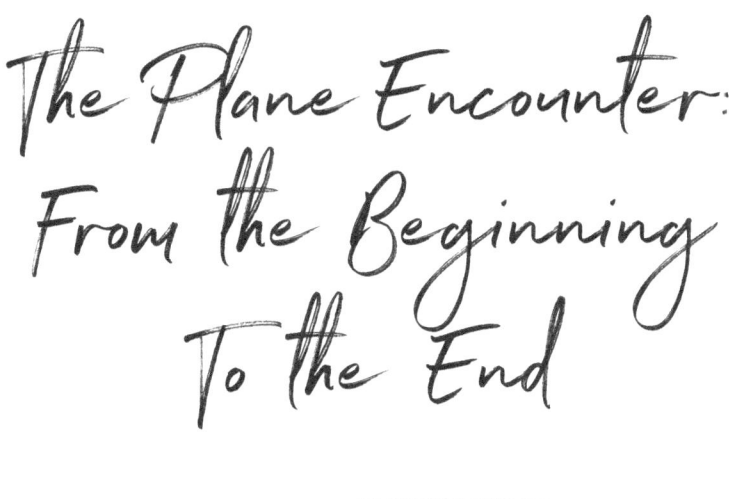

The Plane Encounter: From the Beginning To the End

"But in your hearts revere Christ as Lord. Always be prepared to give an answer to Everyone who asks you to give the reason for the Hope that is in you, with meekness and fear!"

I Peter 3:15

Christmas break during my final year at Baylor University School of Nursing, my parents provided a plane ticket for me to join them in Florida at my grandparents' motel. Excitedly, I packed a suitcase. Throwing in a bathing suit, I glimpsed the small white New Testament that Gideons had presented to all nursing students at Baylor the year before. At the last instant, I tossed it into my purse.

Entering the plane, I found my assigned seat and was a bit dismayed that I had a center seat between two men! "Oh, bother!" I thought as I observed a military guy in the left seat on the aisle and a properly attired business man, briefcase in tow, occupied the window seat. As we taxied and took off, the businessman started the polite chit-chat that attempts to ease an awkward situation of being squeezed between total strangers in economy class.

He asked, "What kind of work do you do?"

"I'm a senior nursing student at Baylor University Medical Center in Dallas, and this month, I am assigned to the oncology ward. You know, it's interesting to hear from patients their views on death," I replied, hoping that would be enough to satisfy him. I was not prepared for his next question:

"So what's your philosophy on death?" Hard swallow. Think, Linda!

I continued, "Well, first I would have to tell you my philosophy on life!" Reaching for that little white New Testament in my purse, I sent up an urgent prayer for the Lord to give me His words! After reading a few verses of the Bible from the book of Romans about all of us being sinners and how Jesus died to reconcile us to God and thereby provide the gift of eternal life, the businessman began to cry and confess his sin of adultery. It felt as if I were standing in front of our row of seats, with a microphone, exclaiming a salvation message to the whole cabin! Passengers were peering between the seats! I was so embarrassed as a 21 year-old single girl that I didn't want to say another word to him.

That's when God took over. Literally.

My mouth continued explaining the way of salvation, that through the death of Jesus on a Roman cross in order to forgive all our sins, God made us acceptable in His sight, so that we could spend eternity in Heaven with Him! All this spoken without any conscious effort on my end. As if God wasn't going to let me mess this up—His plan for this particular man on this particular day. A life was changed for all eternity, praise be to God alone.

We stood to disembark in Atlanta, and the businessman asked me for that little white New Testament. I humbly relinquished it. Before we got off that flight to travel our separate ways, he turned in the aisle to say goodbye and these were his departing words, "There are churches on every corner, but you have done more for me in this past hour than any of them." I would like to know what he did with his new life. I'm hoping his marriage healed.

On the walk to the terminal, the young soldier in uniform tapped me on the shoulder. We conversed for a few minutes inside before going separate ways to catch connecting flights. He told me that he had been raised in a Catholic home and believed in Jesus Christ, but that he had never heard the Gospel explained so plainly and someone so ready to accept it!

That was ALL GOD!

This was the beginning of my journey into missions! Incredible to think that John and I recently returned from a two week retirement cruise from Budapest, Hungary, to Prague, in the Czech Republic—a beautiful voyage. The planning began a year and a half before when my cousin Jeff and his wife Lisa invited us on a Viking River Cruise on the Romantic Danube River in Europe. We were so excited about the wonders of this destination that we invited two more couples: Bruce and Beth and Alan and Holly.

We decided on a departure date of June 2022 and contacted a Viking Vacation Specialist who explained how to make a reservation. Within one month, all of us were "Paid-in-full," a total commitment. Along with our close friends, we added a three-day extended stay in Prague. This part was on us to reserve transportation and lodging so that every detail was confirmed before we ever left home (USA).

Now we could sit back, relax, and enjoy our journey!

Would you ever venture to a country on the other side of the world where the majority would not speak your language without making specific reservations? Just as I asked the business man on another journey, years ago I would like to ask you. Did you know there is a decision for you to make, one you can make here on Earth, that would give you a reservation in Heaven? Do you have any idea where you will spend eternity? Jesus has already paid the expensive price to reserve Heaven for you. He died on a cross to cover your sins and mine in order to make us acceptable to enter God's presence in Heaven. He was buried in a tomb and resurrected on the third day to conquer death for us. Are you ready to trust Jesus to make your reservation to your eternal destination?

LESSON

Be ready at all times!

The Roman Road

The Lord shows us the road and ensures reservations for our journey to Heaven in the Book of Romans:

-Chapter 3, verse 22-23, "The righteousness of God through faith in Jesus Christ for all who believe. For there is no distinction; For all have sinned and fallen short of the glory of God."

-Chapter 6, verse 23, "For the wages of sin is death, but the free gift of God is eternal life in Christ Jesus our Lord."

-Chapter 5, verse 8, "But God shows His love for us in that while we were still sinners, Christ died for us."

-Chapter 10, verses 9-10, "Because if you confess with your mouth that Jesus is Lord and believe in your heart that God raised Him from the dead, you will be saved. For with the heart one believes and is justified, and with the mouth one confesses and is saved."

Meet the Author

 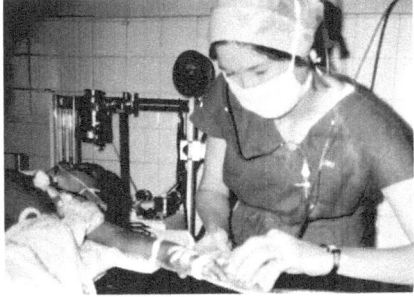

Linda Cox Gibson, received her BSN from Baylor University and an MSN in Nurse Anesthesia from Drexel University of Philadelphia. She married John Gibson, M.D., and moved to Thailand in 1985 where she administered anesthesia in a remote mission hospital (and other hospitals and clinics) for nearly twenty years. She is the mother of Kimberly Dawn and Kaitlyn Diane who grew up in rural Thailand and are fluent in Thai language. She served with her husband under the International Mission Board of the SBC. Singing scripture is her favorite way to memorize God's Word and hide it in her heart. Now retired from clinical practice of forty years, Linda and her husband, John, currently reside in a rain forest in the most northern province of Thailand, with a view of the mountains and green rice fields.